The Power of Productive Learning: Maximizing Your Study Habits

Rowen Julio

Copyright © [2023]

Title: The Power of Productive Learning: Maximizing Your Study Habits
Author's: Rowen Julio

This book was printed and published by [Publisher's: **Rowen Julio**] in [2023]

ISBN:

TABLE OF CONTENT

Chapter 3: Effective Study Techniques for Optimal Learning 20

Chapter 4: Creating a Productive Study Environment 30

Chapter 5: Time Management Strategies for Efficient Study Sessions 38

Prioritizing Tasks and Setting Realistic Goals

Creating a Study Schedule and Sticking to It

Overcoming Procrastination and Avoiding Time Wasters

Balancing Study Time with Other Responsibilities

Chapter 6: Developing Effective Note-Taking Techniques 46

The Cornell Method: A Systematic Approach to Note-Taking

Highlighting and Annotating: Maximizing the Value of Textbooks

Mindful Listening and Note-Taking During Lectures

Incorporating Visual Aids and Diagrams in Note-Taking

Chapter 7: Strategies for Successful Exam Preparation 54

Creating a Study Plan for Exams

Reviewing and Consolidating Course Material

Practicing with Past Exams and Sample Questions

Managing Test Anxiety and Building Confidence

Chapter 8: Overcoming Study Challenges and Adapting to Learning Styles 62

Chapter 9: The Role of Healthy Habits in Enhancing Study Performance 70

Chapter 10: Sustaining Long-Term Study Habits for Lifelong Learning 78

Chapter 1: Understanding the Significance of Study Habits

The Role of Study Habits in Academic Success

As students, we often find ourselves overwhelmed with the demands of academic life. From juggling multiple assignments to preparing for exams, it can be challenging to stay on top of our studies. However, one crucial factor that can significantly impact our academic success is our study habits. In this subchapter, we will explore the importance of proper study habits and how they can maximize our learning potential.

First and foremost, having effective study habits is essential because they provide structure and organization to our learning process. By establishing a routine and sticking to it, we can create a conducive environment for studying. This may involve setting specific study times, creating a quiet and distraction-free space, and having all the necessary materials at hand. When we have a structured approach to studying, we are more likely to manage our time efficiently and avoid procrastination.

Additionally, proper study habits enable us to retain information more effectively. For instance, employing active learning techniques such as summarizing information, creating flashcards, or engaging in group discussions allows us to process and understand the material better. By actively engaging with the content, we enhance our comprehension and memory retention, leading to improved performance in exams and assignments.

Furthermore, study habits contribute to developing strong discipline and self-motivation. Consistently practicing good study habits requires dedication and perseverance. When we stick to our study schedule, even when we don't feel like it, we develop a sense of responsibility and commitment towards our education. This discipline, coupled with self-motivation, drives us to strive for excellence and achieve our academic goals.

Moreover, proper study habits can reduce stress and anxiety associated with studying. When we have a well-structured plan, we feel more in control of our learning process. This reduces the feeling of being overwhelmed and promotes a sense of confidence in our abilities. By managing our time effectively and breaking down complex tasks into smaller, manageable parts, we can approach our studies with a calm and focused mindset.

In conclusion, the role of study habits in academic success cannot be overstated. They provide the necessary structure, enhance comprehension and memory retention, foster discipline and self-motivation, and reduce stress and anxiety. By incorporating effective study habits into our daily routine, we can maximize our learning potential and achieve the academic success we desire.

How Study Habits Impact Learning Efficiency

Introduction:
In today's fast-paced world, students face numerous challenges when it comes to learning effectively. With a myriad of distractions surrounding them, it's crucial for students to understand the importance of proper study habits. This subchapter delves into the impact study habits have on learning efficiency and provides valuable insights to help students maximize their potential.

Understanding Learning Efficiency:
Learning efficiency refers to the ability to acquire and retain knowledge in the most effective manner. It involves a combination of time management, focus, and effective study strategies. The way students approach their studies greatly influences their learning efficiency, which is directly linked to academic success.

The Connection between Study Habits and Learning Efficiency:
Your study habits play a vital role in determining how efficiently you learn. A good study habit involves creating a conducive environment, setting clear goals, managing time effectively, and utilizing effective study techniques. By developing these habits, students can enhance their ability to absorb information, retain it for longer periods, and ultimately perform better in exams.

Creating a Conducive Study Environment:
A clutter-free, well-organized study space is essential for optimal learning. Minimizing distractions such as noise, smartphones, and social media can significantly improve concentration levels. Moreover,

having access to necessary study materials, like textbooks and online resources, within arm's reach can save time and boost productivity.

Setting Clear Goals:
Setting specific, achievable goals allows students to outline what they want to accomplish during their study sessions. By breaking down larger tasks into smaller, manageable ones, students can maintain focus and track their progress. This approach not only enhances learning efficiency but also helps students stay motivated throughout their academic journey.

Time Management:
Effective time management is crucial for maximizing learning efficiency. By allocating specific time slots for studying, students can create a routine that minimizes procrastination and maximizes productivity. Prioritizing tasks based on importance and allocating sufficient breaks also ensures that students maintain focus and prevent burnout.

Utilizing Effective Study Techniques:
Different study techniques work better for different individuals. Experimenting with techniques like active learning, spaced repetition, and self-quizzing can help students identify what works best for them. Incorporating these techniques into their study routine can significantly improve learning efficiency by enhancing comprehension and retention.

Conclusion:
Proper study habits are indispensable for students aiming to achieve academic excellence. By recognizing the impact study habits have on

learning efficiency, students can take control of their education, maximize their potential, and achieve their goals. By creating a conducive study environment, setting clear goals, managing time effectively, and utilizing effective study techniques, students can pave the way for productive and efficient learning.

The Connection Between Study Habits and Retention of Information

In the fast-paced world of education, it is crucial for students to develop effective study habits that maximize their learning potential. The connection between study habits and the retention of information cannot be overstated. It is not enough to simply spend hours studying; rather, it is essential to adopt strategies that enhance comprehension and memory recall. In this subchapter, we will explore the importance of proper study habits and how they can significantly impact academic success.

One key aspect of effective study habits is organization. Students who maintain a well-structured study routine tend to retain information more efficiently. By creating a study schedule, breaking down tasks into manageable chunks, and setting specific goals, students can optimize their learning process. This organization helps to reduce stress and allows for a more focused and productive study session.

Another crucial factor in retaining information is active engagement. Passive reading or mindlessly highlighting textbooks are not effective methods for long-term retention. Instead, students should actively participate in their learning by utilizing techniques such as summarizing information in their own words, creating flashcards, or engaging in group discussions. These activities promote deeper understanding and enhance memory consolidation.

Furthermore, the environment in which students study can greatly impact their retention abilities. A quiet and well-lit space, free from distractions, promotes concentration and improves information retention. It is crucial to find a study environment that works best for each individual, whether it be a library, a coffee shop, or a dedicated study space at home.

Additionally, the utilization of various learning techniques can significantly enhance retention. Visual learners may benefit from incorporating diagrams, charts, or mind maps into their study routine, while auditory learners may find it helpful to record their notes and listen to them later. By tailoring study techniques to individual learning styles, students can maximize their understanding and retention of information.

In conclusion, the connection between study habits and the retention of information is undeniable. By adopting proper study habits, such as organization, active engagement, creating a suitable study environment, and utilizing various learning techniques, students can significantly improve their ability to retain information. These practices not only enhance academic success but also instill valuable skills that can be applied throughout a lifetime of learning.

Chapter 2: Identifying and Assessing Your Current Study Habits

Self-Reflection: Evaluating Your Study Habits

In the journey of academia, it is important to recognize the pivotal role that proper study habits play in achieving academic excellence. Whether you are a high school student preparing for college or a university student aiming for top grades, understanding the importance of effective study habits is crucial. This subchapter aims to guide students towards self-reflection and evaluation of their current study habits, allowing them to make necessary adjustments for maximum productivity.

Self-reflection is a valuable tool that allows individuals to gain insight into their strengths and weaknesses. By taking the time to evaluate your study habits, you can identify areas for improvement and implement strategies that will enhance your learning experience.

Begin this process by asking yourself a series of questions: How do you approach studying? Are you easily distracted? Do you prefer studying alone or in groups? What time of day do you feel most productive? These questions will help you identify any patterns or habits that may be hindering your progress.

Once you have reflected on your current study habits, it is crucial to understand the importance of proper study habits. Effective study habits not only improve academic performance but also foster discipline, time management, and critical thinking skills. By implementing strategies such as creating a study schedule, setting specific goals, and utilizing active learning techniques, you can optimize your learning potential.

It is essential to recognize that everyone has different learning styles and preferences. What works for one student may not work for another. Therefore, it is important to experiment with various study techniques and find what suits you best. Some students thrive in a quiet environment, while others may prefer background music or white noise. By understanding your learning style, you can tailor your study habits to maximize your productivity.

Lastly, self-reflection should be an ongoing process. As you progress in your academic journey, your study habits may require adjustment. Regularly evaluate your habits, identify areas for improvement, and adapt accordingly. Embrace the growth mindset and be open to new strategies that may enhance your learning experience.

In conclusion, self-reflection is key to evaluating and improving your study habits. Recognizing the importance of proper study habits will allow you to develop effective strategies that will enhance your learning experience. By investing time and effort into evaluating and adjusting your study habits, you are setting yourself up for academic success. So, take a moment to reflect, make necessary adjustments, and unlock the power of productive learning.

Recognizing the Strengths and Weaknesses of Your Study Habits

In order to maximize your study habits and become a more productive learner, it is crucial to recognize and understand your individual strengths and weaknesses. By doing so, you can develop strategies that capitalize on your strengths and improve upon your weaknesses, ultimately enhancing your overall learning experience. This subchapter aims to guide students in recognizing their study habits and empowering them to make positive changes.

Firstly, let's discuss the importance of proper study habits. Effective studying is essential for academic success, as it enables students to grasp and retain information more efficiently. By developing good study habits, you can make the most of your study time, improve your understanding of complex subjects, and ultimately achieve higher grades.

To begin assessing your study habits, start by identifying your strengths. These may include your ability to concentrate for extended periods, your aptitude for organizing information, or your skill in managing your time effectively. Recognizing your strengths will allow you to leverage them to your advantage. For example, if you are good at organizing information, you can create visually appealing charts or mind maps to help you remember key concepts.

Next, it is important to be honest with yourself about your weaknesses. Common weaknesses may include procrastination, lack of focus, or struggling to prioritize tasks. Once you identify your weaknesses, you can take steps to address them. For instance, if you struggle with procrastination, you can break your study sessions into smaller, manageable chunks and reward yourself after completing each task.

Furthermore, understanding your learning style is crucial when recognizing your strengths and weaknesses. Some students are visual learners, while others prefer auditory or kinesthetic learning. By identifying your learning style, you can tailor your study techniques accordingly. Visual learners may benefit from using diagrams or flashcards, while auditory learners may find recording lectures helpful.

In conclusion, recognizing the strengths and weaknesses of your study habits is a critical step towards maximizing your learning potential. By understanding what works for you and what doesn't, you can develop strategies that align with your strengths and address your weaknesses. This subchapter has provided an overview of the importance of proper study habits and highlighted the significance of self-assessment in improving your study skills. By taking the time to evaluate your study habits, you are empowering yourself to become a more efficient and productive learner.

Tools for Assessing Your Study Habits

In order to maximize your study habits and achieve academic success, it is crucial to assess and evaluate your current study practices. This subchapter will introduce you to various tools that can help you gain a deeper understanding of your study habits and identify areas for improvement. By using these tools, you will be able to adopt more effective and efficient study techniques, ultimately enhancing your learning experience.

One of the most valuable tools for assessing your study habits is a study log or journal. This simple yet powerful tool allows you to track and record your study sessions, including the duration, subjects covered, and the methods you employed. By regularly documenting your study habits, you can analyze patterns and trends, such as the times of day when you are most productive or the subjects that require more attention. This self-reflection will enable you to make informed decisions about how to optimize your study routine.

Another useful tool is a self-assessment questionnaire. These questionnaires are designed to evaluate your study skills, time management, concentration, and motivation levels. They provide a comprehensive overview of your strengths and weaknesses, allowing you to identify areas that require improvement. By honestly answering these questions, you can gain valuable insights into your study habits and make necessary adjustments to achieve better results.

Additionally, online learning platforms and apps can offer valuable insights into your study habits. Many of these tools provide analytics and reports, which analyze your study patterns and performance. They can track the time you spend on different tasks, identify distractions, and even suggest personalized study plans based on your learning style. By utilizing these tools, you can take advantage of data-driven insights to enhance your study habits and optimize your academic performance.

Lastly, seeking feedback from teachers, peers, or academic advisors can provide valuable perspectives on your study habits. They can offer insights into areas you may have overlooked and provide strategies for improvement. Their guidance and constructive criticism can help you refine your study habits and achieve your academic goals.

In conclusion, assessing your study habits is essential for maximizing your learning potential. By utilizing tools such as study logs, self-assessment questionnaires, online platforms, and seeking feedback, you can gain a deeper understanding of your study habits and make necessary adjustments for improvement. By adopting effective study techniques, you will be able to enhance your learning experience and achieve academic success. Remember, proper study habits are the key to unlocking your true potential.

Chapter 3: Effective Study Techniques for Optimal Learning

The Pomodoro Technique: Enhancing Focus and Productivity

In the fast-paced world of academia, it is crucial for students to develop effective study habits that can boost their focus and productivity. One such technique that has gained popularity among students is the Pomodoro Technique. This subchapter will explore how this technique can be a game-changer in enhancing your study habits.

The Pomodoro Technique is a time management method developed by Francesco Cirillo in the late 1980s. The concept behind this technique is simple yet powerful - breaking your study time into manageable intervals, typically 25 minutes, called "Pomodoros," with short breaks in between. These intervals are designed to maximize concentration and prevent burnout.

One of the key advantages of the Pomodoro Technique is that it combats the tendency to procrastinate. By setting a timer for a specific period, you create a sense of urgency and eliminate distractions. This focused approach allows you to dive deep into your studies and make the most of your time.

Moreover, the Pomodoro Technique helps you maintain a healthy work-life balance. By incorporating short breaks between each Pomodoro, you give your mind a chance to rest and recharge. Stepping away from your studies for a few minutes can actually improve your ability to retain information and boost your overall productivity.

Another benefit of the Pomodoro Technique is that it promotes time awareness and task prioritization. By allocating specific time slots for different subjects or tasks, you can better manage your study schedule. This technique encourages you to allocate more time to challenging subjects while ensuring that you cover all the necessary material.

Implementing the Pomodoro Technique requires discipline and commitment. It is important to find a quiet and comfortable study environment, free from distractions. Additionally, using a timer or a Pomodoro app can help you stay on track and monitor your progress.

In conclusion, the Pomodoro Technique is a valuable tool for students aiming to enhance their focus and productivity. By breaking your study time into manageable intervals and incorporating short breaks, you can combat procrastination, maintain a healthy work-life balance, and improve time management skills. Give this technique a try and witness the positive impact it can have on your study habits.

Active Reading Strategies for Improved Comprehension

Introduction:

In this subchapter, we will explore the concept of active reading strategies and how they can significantly enhance your comprehension skills. As students, it is crucial to develop effective study habits to fully grasp the material and excel academically. By implementing these strategies, you can unlock the power of productive learning and make the most of your study sessions.

1.   Previewing   the   Material:
Before diving into a text, take a few minutes to preview it. Skim through the headings, subheadings, and bolded or italicized text. This will provide you with an overview of the content, helping you create a mental framework and anticipate what to expect.

2.   Asking   Questions:
As you read, actively engage with the material by asking yourself questions. This stimulates critical thinking and promotes active learning. Consider the main ideas, supporting evidence, and how the information relates to what you already know. By seeking answers to these questions, you will improve your comprehension and memory retention.

3.   Highlighting   and   Annotating:
Highlighting key points and annotating the text is an effective way to interact with the material. Use different colors to differentiate between main ideas, supporting details, and examples. Additionally, jot down your thoughts, summaries, and connections in the margins. These

annotations will serve as valuable study aids when reviewing the material later.

4.   Summarizing:
After reading a section or chapter, challenge yourself to summarize the main points in your own words. This exercise not only reinforces comprehension but also helps consolidate your knowledge. By distilling complex concepts into concise summaries, you strengthen your grasp of the material and make it easier to recall when needed.

5.   Visualizing:
Engage your imagination by visualizing the concepts or information you are reading. Create mental images or diagrams to represent the ideas and relationships between them. Visual aids can enhance comprehension, as they provide a visual anchor that aids memory recall.

Conclusion:
Incorporating active reading strategies into your study routine is a game-changer. These techniques allow you to actively engage with the material, enhancing comprehension and retention. By previewing, questioning, highlighting, summarizing, and visualizing, you will maximize your study habits and unlock the power of productive learning. Remember, proper study habits are essential for academic success, and active reading is a vital component of this process.

Mind Mapping: Organizing Information for Better Understanding

In today's fast-paced and information-driven world, students face a constant challenge when it comes to organizing and understanding the vast amount of knowledge they need to acquire. Proper study habits play a crucial role in ensuring academic success and maximizing learning potential. One effective technique that can revolutionize the way you approach studying is mind mapping.

Mind mapping is a visual tool that helps students organize information in a structured and engaging manner. It allows you to create a visual representation of concepts, topics, and ideas, making it easier to grasp complex information. By using colors, images, and keywords, mind maps stimulate both the left and right sides of the brain, enhancing memory retention and recall.

One key advantage of mind mapping is its ability to capture the interconnectedness of ideas. Traditional note-taking methods often lead to linear and disconnected information, making it challenging to see the bigger picture. However, mind maps enable you to identify relationships, patterns, and hierarchies between different concepts. This holistic approach promotes a deeper understanding of the subject matter and enhances critical thinking skills.

Moreover, mind mapping can help students unlock their creativity. By incorporating visual elements and personalizing your mind maps, you can tap into your creative side and make studying a more enjoyable experience. This technique encourages active engagement with the material, making it easier to remember and apply knowledge in exams and real-life situations.

To create a mind map, start by identifying the main topic or subject you want to study. Write it down in the center of a blank page and draw branches radiating from it like the branches of a tree. Each branch represents a subtopic or main idea related to the central concept. Use keywords, images, and colors to represent each idea and connect them with lines to indicate relationships.

As you continue to build your mind map, don't be afraid to revise and refine it. Mind mapping is a dynamic process that allows for flexibility and adaptability. You can add new branches, expand on existing ones, or rearrange the layout to suit your evolving understanding of the subject.

In conclusion, mind mapping is a powerful tool that can transform your study habits and enhance your learning experience. By organizing information in a visually appealing and interconnected manner, you will not only improve your understanding but also boost your creativity and critical thinking skills. Incorporate mind mapping into your study routine and unlock your full learning potential.

The Feynman Technique: Mastering Concepts Through Simplification

Proper study habits are essential for any student who aims to succeed academically. In today's fast-paced and information-driven world, students are often overwhelmed with complex concepts and topics. However, there is a powerful technique that can help you not only understand these concepts but also master them - The Feynman Technique.

Named after the renowned physicist Richard Feynman, this technique is designed to simplify complex ideas and make them easier to comprehend. The core principle of the Feynman Technique is to teach someone else the concept you are trying to learn. By explaining a concept in simple terms, you will be able to identify any gaps in your understanding and fill them in.

To implement the Feynman Technique, begin by choosing a concept you want to learn. Break it down into smaller components and try to explain each one in your own words. Pretend that you are teaching someone who has no prior knowledge of the subject, and use simple language to convey your explanations. If you find yourself struggling to explain a certain aspect, it indicates that you need to revisit that particular area and deepen your understanding.

Another crucial step in the Feynman Technique is to identify and eliminate jargon. Often, complex subjects are filled with technical terms and specialized vocabulary that can be confusing. By simplifying these terms and explaining them in everyday language, you will be able to grasp the concept more effectively.

Additionally, visual aids can be invaluable when using the Feynman Technique. Diagrams, charts, or illustrations can help you visualize the concept and make it more tangible. This visual representation will not only enhance your understanding but also make it easier to explain to others.

The Feynman Technique is a powerful tool that has proven to be highly effective in mastering complex concepts. By simplifying ideas and teaching them to others, you will not only solidify your own understanding but also gain the ability to explain those concepts to classmates, friends, or even yourself. So, the next time you encounter a challenging topic, try applying the Feynman Technique and watch your understanding soar to new heights.

Utilizing Flashcards and Mnemonics for Memorization

In the fast-paced world of academia, students often find themselves overwhelmed with an abundance of information that needs to be memorized. Whether it's historical dates, scientific formulas, or foreign language vocabulary, the ability to retain and recall information is crucial for success. This is where the power of flashcards and mnemonics comes into play.

Flashcards are a versatile and effective tool that can be used to aid in the memorization process. They provide a simple yet powerful way to break down complex concepts into bite-sized pieces of information. By writing a question or a keyword on one side and the corresponding answer or definition on the other, flashcards encourage active recall and help reinforce learning. The repetitive nature of reviewing flashcards strengthens neural connections, making it easier for the brain to retrieve information when needed.

To enhance the effectiveness of flashcards, incorporating mnemonics can be a game-changer. Mnemonics are memory aids that use associations or visualization techniques to help remember information. For example, creating acronyms, rhymes, or visual images can make abstract concepts more concrete and memorable. By linking new information to familiar or vivid imagery, the brain is more likely to retain and recall it when necessary.

When utilizing flashcards and mnemonics for memorization, it is essential to adopt a systematic approach. Start by creating a set of flashcards for the topic you wish to learn. Break down the information into smaller, manageable chunks. Write clear and concise questions or keywords on one side of each card, ensuring they cover the key points you want to memorize. On the other side, provide detailed answers or definitions.

Next, introduce mnemonics into the learning process. Find creative ways to associate the information on the flashcards with memorable mental images or catchy phrases. Experiment with different mnemonic techniques to discover which ones work best for you. Keep in mind that mnemonics should be personalized and tailored to your learning style and preferences.

Consistent and regular practice with flashcards and mnemonics is vital for long-term retention. Allocate dedicated study sessions to review your flashcards, preferably in spaced intervals to reinforce learning. By repeatedly testing your memory and actively engaging with the material, you will strengthen your recall abilities and develop a solid foundation of knowledge.

In conclusion, flashcards and mnemonics are invaluable tools in the quest for effective memorization. By incorporating these techniques into your study routine, you can enhance your learning experience and maximize your study habits. Embrace the power of flashcards and mnemonics, and unlock your true potential as a student.

Chapter 4: Creating a Productive Study Environment

Setting Up a Distraction-Free Space

Creating an ideal study environment is crucial for maximizing your learning potential. In today's world filled with countless distractions, it is essential to have a dedicated space that allows you to focus and concentrate on your studies. This subchapter will guide you through the process of setting up a distraction-free space, ensuring that your study sessions are productive and efficient.

Step 1: Choose the Right Location
The first step in setting up a distraction-free space is selecting the right location. Find a quiet area in your home or dormitory where you can study without being disturbed. It could be a spare room, a corner of your bedroom, or even a quiet corner in the library. Ensure that the space is well-lit and has good ventilation to keep you feeling alert and oxygenated.

Step 2: Eliminate Distractions
Identify the potential distractions in your chosen study space and eliminate them as much as possible. Keep your phone on silent or in a different room to avoid the temptation of checking social media or answering calls. If you are studying on your computer, use website blockers or apps that limit access to distracting websites. Clear your study area of unnecessary clutter and remove any items that may divert your attention.

Step 3: Organize Your Supplies
Having all your study materials within reach will help you stay

focused. Organize your supplies, such as textbooks, notebooks, pens, and highlighters, in a neat and accessible manner. Use bookshelves, desk organizers, or storage boxes to keep everything in order. This will minimize the time spent searching for materials and maximize your study efficiency.

Step 4: Create a Comfortable Workspace
Comfort is essential for long study sessions. Invest in a good quality chair that provides proper back support and a desk at an appropriate height to prevent any discomfort or strain. Consider adding a plant or some artwork to make the space more visually appealing and conducive to learning. Ensure that the temperature in the room is comfortable, as extreme temperatures can negatively affect your concentration.

Step 5: Set Study Goals and Boundaries
Before starting your study session, set clear goals for what you want to achieve. Break your study time into manageable chunks, with short breaks in between to rest and recharge. Establish boundaries with those around you, letting them know that during your designated study time, you should not be disturbed unless it is an emergency.

By setting up a distraction-free space, you are creating an environment that promotes focused and effective learning. Implement these steps, and you will notice a significant improvement in your study habits and academic performance. Remember, a conducive study environment is a powerful tool in harnessing the power of productive learning.

Optimizing Lighting and Noise Levels for Concentration

When it comes to studying effectively, creating the right environment is crucial. Two factors that significantly impact your ability to concentrate are lighting and noise levels. In this subchapter, we will delve into the importance of optimizing these elements to enhance your study habits and maximize your learning potential.

Lighting plays a vital role in maintaining focus and preventing eye strain. Natural light is ideal, as it provides a sense of alertness and promotes a positive mood. If possible, position your study area near a window to allow for ample sunlight. However, if natural light is limited, opt for a bright, white light source that mimics daylight. Avoid harsh, fluorescent lighting as it can cause headaches and fatigue. Additionally, ensure that your workspace is well-lit, eliminating any shadows that may strain your eyes.

On the other hand, noise levels can either aid or hinder your concentration. While some individuals thrive in complete silence, others find a moderate level of background noise to be beneficial. Experiment with different options to discover what works best for you. If you prefer a quiet environment, find a secluded spot in your home or utilize noise-cancelling headphones to block out distractions. Alternatively, if you find a bit of noise helpful, ambient sounds such as instrumental music or white noise can create a soothing backdrop and drown out any disruptive sounds.

Creating an atmosphere conducive to concentration goes beyond lighting and noise control. Keep your study area organized, as clutter can be a significant source of distraction. A clean workspace promotes a clear mind and allows you to focus solely on your studies. Remove any unnecessary items from your desk and keep only the essentials within reach.

Moreover, consider the ergonomics of your study space. Invest in a comfortable chair with proper back support to prevent discomfort and potential health issues. Keep your monitor at eye level to avoid strain on your neck and eyes. Taking care of your physical well-being while studying will enhance your overall productivity and prevent unnecessary fatigue.

By optimizing lighting and noise levels and creating a conducive study environment, you can greatly improve your concentration and maximize your learning potential. Remember that everyone is unique, so it is essential to experiment and find what works best for you. By incorporating these strategies into your study routine, you will be well on your way to unlocking the power of productive learning.

Organizing Study Materials for Easy Access

In the quest to become more productive learners, it is crucial for students to develop effective study habits. One of the most overlooked aspects of studying is organizing study materials for easy access. This subchapter will delve into the importance of organizing study materials and provide practical tips for students to implement in their daily study routines.

Proper organization of study materials is paramount for several reasons. Firstly, it saves valuable time. When study materials are scattered or disorganized, students waste precious minutes searching for the right notes or textbooks. By having a systematic approach to organizing materials, students can easily locate the resources they need, allowing them to focus their energy on actual studying.

Secondly, organizing study materials enhances retention and understanding. When notes, textbooks, and other resources are arranged in a logical manner, it becomes easier to review and connect information. This systematic approach aids in the creation of mental frameworks, facilitating better understanding and retention of the subject matter.

To implement effective organization strategies, students should start by decluttering their study spaces. Remove any unnecessary items that may distract or hinder concentration. Invest in storage solutions such as shelves, file folders, and binders to keep materials tidy and easily accessible.

Creating a labeling system is another valuable technique. Labeling notebooks, folders, and digital files with clear and specific titles will help students quickly identify the content they need. Color-coding can also be employed, assigning different colors to different subjects or topics. This visual distinction further enhances accessibility and streamlines the studying process.

Digital organization tools can also prove helpful. Utilize note-taking apps, such as Evernote or OneNote, to store and categorize digital notes. These apps allow students to easily search for specific keywords or topics, saving time and effort.

Regularly reviewing and maintaining the organization system is essential. As study materials accumulate, it is important to periodically reassess and reorganize. This ensures that the system remains efficient and clutter-free.

In conclusion, organizing study materials for easy access is a vital component of developing productive study habits. By implementing effective organization strategies, students can save time, enhance understanding, and improve retention. Decluttering study spaces, creating labeling systems, and utilizing digital tools are all practical tips that can help students streamline their studying process. So, take the time to organize your study materials and unlock the power of productive learning.

Utilizing Technology for Effective Study

In today's digital age, technology has become an integral part of our lives, transforming the way we communicate, work, and even learn. As students, it is crucial to adapt and harness the power of technology to enhance our study habits and maximize our learning potential. This subchapter explores the various ways in which technology can be utilized effectively for studying, offering valuable insights and tips to help students excel academically.

One of the key benefits of technology in studying is the easy access to a wealth of information. The internet provides a vast repository of knowledge, allowing students to conduct research, explore different perspectives, and find relevant resources for their assignments and projects. Online libraries, scholarly databases, and educational websites serve as invaluable tools for expanding our understanding and deepening our knowledge in any subject matter.

Furthermore, technology offers numerous tools and applications that aid in organization and time management. With the help of productivity apps, students can create to-do lists, set reminders, and track their progress. These tools enable us to stay focused, prioritize tasks, and allocate our study time efficiently. By utilizing technology for effective time management, students can strike a balance between their academic responsibilities and other aspects of their lives.

Collaboration and communication are also greatly enhanced through technology. Online platforms, such as discussion forums and virtual study groups, enable students to connect with their peers, exchange ideas, and collaborate on projects even when physically apart. This fosters a sense of community and facilitates collective learning, as students can benefit from diverse perspectives and engage in meaningful discussions with their peers.

Moreover, technology offers innovative ways to engage with course material and enhance retention. Interactive learning platforms, educational apps, and multimedia resources provide immersive and interactive experiences, making the learning process more engaging and enjoyable. Visual representations, videos, and simulations can help clarify complex concepts and aid in knowledge retention.

It is important to note, however, that while technology can greatly enhance our study habits, it is crucial to use it judiciously and avoid distractions. It is essential to establish boundaries and create a conducive environment for studying, free from unnecessary interruptions. Balance is key – technology should be seen as a tool to aid learning, not as a distraction that hinders our academic progress.

In conclusion, the effective utilization of technology has the potential to revolutionize our study habits and maximize our learning potential. By harnessing the power of technology, students can access information easily, manage their time effectively, collaborate with peers, and engage with course material in innovative ways. Embracing technology as a valuable study tool will undoubtedly enhance our academic journey and empower us to become more productive and successful students.

Chapter 5: Time Management Strategies for Efficient Study Sessions

Prioritizing Tasks and Setting Realistic Goals

One crucial aspect of developing effective study habits is learning how to prioritize tasks and set realistic goals. As students, we often find ourselves juggling multiple assignments, projects, and extracurricular activities, which can quickly become overwhelming if not managed properly. By understanding the importance of prioritization and goal-setting, we can maximize our productivity and achieve academic success.

To begin with, prioritizing tasks allows us to focus our time and energy on the most important and urgent assignments. By identifying which tasks require immediate attention, we can ensure that we complete them in a timely manner, thus avoiding the stress of last-minute rushes. Prioritization also helps us allocate our resources effectively, enabling us to dedicate more time to challenging subjects or assignments that require deeper understanding.

When it comes to setting realistic goals, it is important to remember that we are only human and have limitations. By setting achievable goals, we can maintain a sense of motivation and avoid feeling overwhelmed or discouraged. Unrealistic goals, on the other hand, may lead to burnout and hinder our overall progress. By breaking larger tasks into smaller, manageable goals, we can track our progress and celebrate small victories along the way.

Another benefit of setting realistic goals is that it helps us stay focused and organized. By having a clear vision of what we want to achieve, we can structure our study sessions accordingly, making the most of our time. For instance, if we know that we have a long-term project due at the end of the semester, we can break it down into smaller milestones and dedicate specific study sessions to each milestone. This approach not only ensures steady progress but also helps us stay on track and avoid procrastination.

In conclusion, prioritizing tasks and setting realistic goals are essential components of effective study habits. By mastering these skills, students can overcome the challenges of academic life and maximize their productivity. Prioritization allows us to focus on important tasks, while goal-setting keeps us motivated and organized. By implementing these strategies, we can unlock the power of productive learning and achieve our academic goals.

Creating a Study Schedule and Sticking to It

In today's fast-paced world, proper study habits are crucial for students to excel academically. Without effective strategies in place, it is easy to fall behind and feel overwhelmed with the amount of information that needs to be absorbed. One of the key ways to establish a successful study routine is by creating a study schedule and, more importantly, sticking to it.

A study schedule provides structure and helps to prioritize tasks, ensuring that every subject and topic receives adequate attention. It allows students to allocate specific time slots for studying each day, preventing procrastination and promoting consistency. By following a well-planned schedule, students can make the most of their study time and retain information more effectively.

To create a study schedule, start by assessing your personal preferences and learning style. Some students may find it beneficial to study in shorter, focused bursts, while others may prefer longer study sessions. Consider your energy levels throughout the day and identify the periods when you are most alert and focused. This will help you determine the optimal study times for each subject.

Once you have determined your study preferences, allocate specific time slots for each subject or topic. Break down larger subjects into manageable chunks and assign them to different days or weeks, depending on their complexity and importance. This will ensure that you cover all necessary material without feeling overwhelmed.

Remember to incorporate breaks into your study schedule. Short breaks between study sessions can help refresh your mind and prevent burnout. Use this time to engage in activities that relax and recharge you, such as taking a walk, listening to music, or practicing mindfulness exercises. By incorporating breaks into your schedule, you will maintain your focus and productivity.

However, creating a study schedule alone is not enough; sticking to it is equally important. Discipline and commitment are key factors in making your study routine successful. Avoid distractions by turning off your phone or finding a quiet place to study. Inform your friends and family about your study schedule, so they can support you and respect your dedicated study time.

Remember, the purpose of creating a study schedule is to establish good study habits that will benefit you in the long run. Stay committed to your schedule, adjust it as needed, and be flexible when unexpected circumstances arise. By creating a study schedule and sticking to it, you will not only improve your academic performance but also develop valuable time management skills that will serve you well throughout your life.

Overcoming Procrastination and Avoiding Time Wasters

Procrastination is a common challenge that many students face when it comes to studying. It is the act of delaying or postponing tasks, often leading to unnecessary stress and poor performance. In this subchapter, we will explore effective strategies to overcome procrastination and avoid time wasters, allowing you to maximize your study habits and achieve academic success.

One of the most crucial steps in overcoming procrastination is understanding its root causes. Procrastination can stem from various factors such as fear of failure, lack of motivation, or feeling overwhelmed by the workload. Identifying these underlying reasons will help you develop targeted strategies to combat them.

One effective method to overcome procrastination is to break down your tasks into smaller, manageable chunks. By setting specific and achievable goals, you can eliminate the feeling of being overwhelmed and increase your sense of accomplishment. Create a study schedule and prioritize your tasks based on their importance and urgency. This will enable you to allocate sufficient time for each task, preventing last-minute cramming and stress.

Another helpful technique is to eliminate distractions and create a conducive study environment. Turn off notifications on your phone, limit access to social media, and find a quiet place where you can concentrate. Minimizing external disturbances will enhance your focus and productivity. Consider using productivity apps or website blockers to stay on track and avoid falling into the trap of time-wasting activities.

Effective time management is crucial in avoiding procrastination. Learn to differentiate between important and non-essential tasks. Prioritize your studies over leisure activities and be disciplined in adhering to your study schedule. Additionally, utilize time management techniques such as the Pomodoro Technique, where you study in focused bursts followed by short breaks. This method helps maintain your concentration and prevents burnout.

Lastly, remember to reward yourself for completing tasks and achieving your goals. Celebrate your accomplishments to stay motivated and reinforce positive study habits. Engaging in activities you enjoy during breaks can also serve as a source of motivation.

By implementing these strategies, you can overcome procrastination, avoid time wasters, and develop productive study habits. Remember, effective time management and discipline are the keys to academic success. Start today and unlock the power of productive learning!

Balancing Study Time with Other Responsibilities

As students, we often find ourselves struggling to juggle our academic responsibilities with the numerous other commitments we have in our lives. From extracurricular activities to part-time jobs and social obligations, it can be challenging to strike a balance between study time and everything else. However, it is crucial to understand the importance of managing our time effectively and establishing proper study habits to maximize our learning potential.

One of the key aspects of achieving this balance is creating a schedule that accommodates both study time and other responsibilities. By allocating specific time slots for studying and sticking to them, we can ensure that we dedicate enough hours to our academic pursuits without neglecting our other commitments. This requires discipline and dedication, as it can be tempting to procrastinate or prioritize other activities over studying. However, by adhering to a well-structured schedule, we can develop a routine that allows us to fulfill our obligations while still making progress in our studies.

Another valuable strategy for balancing study time with other responsibilities is learning how to prioritize effectively. It is essential to identify which tasks are most urgent or have the highest impact on our academic success. By focusing on these priorities first, we can make the most efficient use of our study time and ensure that we are dedicating our energy to the tasks that matter the most. This may require making difficult choices and occasionally saying no to certain activities or commitments that do not align with our academic goals. However, by setting clear priorities, we can maintain a healthy balance and avoid feeling overwhelmed by our workload.

Furthermore, it is important to recognize the significance of self-care and rest in maintaining a productive study routine. While it may seem counterintuitive, taking regular breaks and allowing ourselves time to relax and recharge can actually enhance our ability to absorb information and retain knowledge. By incorporating short breaks into our study sessions and ensuring we get enough sleep and exercise, we can optimize our brain function and improve our overall productivity.

In conclusion, balancing study time with other responsibilities is a crucial skill for students to develop. By creating a well-structured schedule, prioritizing effectively, and taking care of our well-being, we can maximize our study habits and achieve academic success while still fulfilling our other obligations. It is important to remember that finding this balance requires discipline, but the rewards of effective time management and productive learning habits are well worth the effort.

Chapter 6: Developing Effective Note-Taking Techniques

The Cornell Method: A Systematic Approach to Note-Taking

Subchapter: The Cornell Method: A Systematic Approach to Note-Taking

Effective note-taking is a crucial skill for students to develop, as it enhances learning and comprehension. One popular and proven method that can revolutionize your note-taking experience is the Cornell Method. This systematic approach not only organizes your notes but also helps you review and retain information effectively. In this subchapter, we will delve into the Cornell Method and explore how it can improve your study habits.

The Cornell Method, developed by Walter Pauk at Cornell University, is a simple yet powerful technique that involves dividing your note sheet into three distinct sections: the cue column, the notes column, and the summary section. This method encourages active learning and engages your brain in the process of synthesizing information.

The cue column is located on the left side of the page and is used to generate questions or keywords related to the content. As you listen to lectures or read textbooks, jot down relevant cues that trigger your memory. These cues act as a roadmap to guide you during review sessions and provide a quick overview of the main topics.

The notes column, situated on the right side, is where you record detailed information. Focus on capturing key ideas, supporting evidence, and examples. Use abbreviations, symbols, and diagrams to condense information without losing its meaning. Aim for clarity and coherence, as well-organized notes facilitate comprehension and revision.

The summary section, located at the bottom of the page, is crucial for reflection and review. After completing your notes, take a few minutes to summarize the main points discussed. This process reinforces your understanding and aids in long-term retention. Additionally, the summary section serves as a valuable resource when reviewing for exams or writing papers.

The Cornell Method offers several benefits. Firstly, it promotes active engagement with the material, ensuring that you remain focused and attentive. Secondly, it provides a structured framework for organizing information, making it easier to identify key concepts and connections. Lastly, the method facilitates effective review by condensing content into concise cues and summaries.

By adopting the Cornell Method, you can transform your note-taking experience and maximize your study habits. This systematic approach will not only enhance your understanding of the subject matter but also improve your academic performance. So, grab a pen and paper, and start implementing this powerful technique today. Your future self will thank you.

Highlighting and Annotating: Maximizing the Value of Textbooks

In today's fast-paced academic environment, it is crucial for students to develop effective study habits that can propel them towards success. One such habit that holds immense value is the art of highlighting and annotating textbooks. This subchapter aims to shed light on the importance of this practice and how it can maximize the value of your textbooks.

When it comes to studying, textbooks are an indispensable tool. However, simply reading through the material is not enough to fully grasp and retain the information. Highlighting and annotating, on the other hand, actively engage your mind and promote deeper understanding. By marking essential points, key concepts, and relevant examples, you create a visual roadmap within the text that helps you navigate through the material with ease.

Not only does highlighting and annotating enhance your comprehension, but it also serves as a powerful revision tool. When you revisit the text, your annotations act as valuable cues, allowing you to swiftly locate and review crucial information. This method not only saves time but also solidifies your understanding, ensuring that the knowledge is firmly embedded in your long-term memory.

Furthermore, through highlighting and annotating, you can personalize your textbooks to suit your learning style. Everyone has their unique way of processing information, and by adding your thoughts, questions, and connections within the margins, you create a personalized learning experience. This active interaction with the material fosters a deeper connection with the subject matter, making it easier to recall and apply the knowledge later on.

To get the most out of your highlighting and annotating practice, it is essential to develop a systematic approach. Start by skimming through the chapter, identifying headings, subheadings, and any important keywords. As you delve deeper into the content, use different colors to highlight main ideas, supporting evidence, and definitions. Alongside the highlighting, jot down concise notes, summaries, and questions in the margins. This approach will enable you to extract the essence of the text and create a concise summary that can be revisited effortlessly.

In conclusion, highlighting and annotating textbooks is a powerful study habit that can significantly enhance your learning experience. By actively engaging with the material, you deepen your understanding, create a personalized learning experience, and improve information retention. So, embrace this practice, and unlock the full potential of your textbooks to maximize your academic success.

Mindful Listening and Note-Taking During Lectures

In the fast-paced world of academia, it is easy for students to become overwhelmed with the amount of information presented during lectures. However, the key to effective learning lies in developing proper study habits, such as mindful listening and note-taking. These techniques not only improve comprehension but also aid in retaining information for future use.

Mindful listening is the art of actively engaging with the material being presented. It involves being fully present, paying attention to the speaker, and focusing on the key points. By actively listening, students can better understand the concepts being discussed and make meaningful connections with their prior knowledge. This practice not only enhances comprehension but also encourages critical thinking and analysis.

Another vital aspect of mindful listening is taking accurate and organized notes. Note-taking allows students to capture important information, key ideas, and supporting details during lectures. It acts as a personalized study tool that can be referred to later, helping students review and reinforce their understanding of the subject matter. Effective note-taking involves using a combination of concise phrases, bullet points, and diagrams to condense complex information into easily digestible chunks.

To maximize the benefits of mindful listening and note-taking, students should adopt certain strategies. First, they should come prepared to class by reviewing the previous lecture's notes and skimming through the relevant reading material. This preparation helps students familiarize themselves with the topic, making it easier to follow along during the lecture.

During the lecture, students should actively participate by asking questions, seeking clarification, and engaging in discussions. This not only demonstrates their attentiveness but also enhances their understanding by interacting with the material in real-time.

Furthermore, it is essential to review and revise lecture notes regularly. This practice reinforces learning, strengthens memory retention, and helps identify any gaps in understanding. By reviewing notes soon after the lecture and periodically throughout the semester, students can maintain a solid grasp of the material.

In conclusion, mindful listening and note-taking are crucial study habits that can significantly improve academic performance. By actively engaging with the material, taking accurate notes, and regularly reviewing them, students can enhance comprehension, retain information, and maximize their learning potential. These techniques are invaluable tools that empower students to make the most of their educational journey.

Incorporating Visual Aids and Diagrams in Note-Taking

Visual aids and diagrams have long been recognized as powerful tools for enhancing learning and memory retention. As students, it is crucial to understand the significance of incorporating these aids in our note-taking process. In this subchapter, we will delve into the reasons why visual aids and diagrams are essential for effective study habits.

First and foremost, visual aids help to simplify complex information. When we encounter intricate concepts or ideas, it can be challenging to grasp them solely through text-based notes. However, by incorporating visual aids such as charts, graphs, or diagrams, we can visually represent the information and make it more comprehensible. Visuals can break down complex ideas into smaller, manageable parts, making it easier for our brains to process and retain the information.

Moreover, visual aids enhance the organization and structure of our notes. When we take textual notes, they often appear as a series of disconnected thoughts and ideas. However, by incorporating visual aids, we can create a clear hierarchy and relationship between different pieces of information. For instance, using flowcharts or mind maps can help outline the connections between different concepts, enabling us to see the bigger picture and understand how everything fits together.

Visual aids also stimulate creativity and engagement during the studying process. By utilizing colors, symbols, and images, we can make our notes more visually appealing, which in turn enhances our motivation to study. Additionally, the act of creating visual aids encourages active learning, as it requires us to actively process and synthesize information rather than passively copying it down. This active engagement helps to reinforce our understanding and retention of the material.

Lastly, visual aids and diagrams are excellent tools for revision and review. When it comes time to study for exams or review material for assignments, visual aids provide a quick and efficient way to jog our memory. Instead of reading through pages of text, we can glance at a diagram or chart and instantly recall the associated information.

In conclusion, incorporating visual aids and diagrams in our note-taking process is vital for effective study habits. These aids simplify complex information, enhance organization, stimulate creativity and engagement, and facilitate revision and review. By embracing the power of visual aids, we can maximize our study habits, improve our understanding, and achieve academic success.

Chapter 7: Strategies for Successful Exam Preparation

Creating a Study Plan for Exams

In order to achieve success in your academic journey, it is crucial to develop proper study habits. The importance of adopting effective study techniques cannot be overstated, as they can significantly enhance your learning experience and help you excel in exams. One of the most effective ways to cultivate productive study habits is by creating a well-organized and comprehensive study plan.

A study plan serves as a roadmap for your learning journey, ensuring that you cover all the necessary material and allocate sufficient time to each subject. By following a study plan, you can avoid last-minute cramming and reduce stress levels, ultimately leading to better performance in exams. Here are some steps to help you create an effective study plan:

1. Assess your strengths and weaknesses: Begin by evaluating your current knowledge and understanding of each subject. Identify areas where you excel and those that require more attention. This self-assessment will help you prioritize your study time accordingly.

2. Set realistic goals: Determine what you aim to achieve through your study plan. Set specific, measurable, attainable, relevant, and time-bound (SMART) goals for each subject. This will help you stay focused and motivated throughout your study sessions.

3. Break it down: Divide your study material into manageable chunks. Create a timetable that allocates sufficient time for each subject,

ensuring that you cover all necessary topics. Consider your personal preferences and energy levels when scheduling study sessions.

4. Prioritize and allocate time: Prioritize subjects based on their importance or difficulty level. Allocate more time to challenging subjects while ensuring that you dedicate sufficient time to all subjects. Remember to include breaks in your timetable to maintain focus and prevent burnout.

5. Use effective study techniques: Experiment with various study techniques, such as active recall, summarizing, and concept mapping, to find the methods that work best for you. Incorporate these techniques into your study plan to enhance retention and understanding.

6. Review and revise: Regularly review your study plan and make adjustments as needed. Be flexible and adaptable, allowing your plan to evolve based on your progress and changing needs.

By creating a comprehensive study plan, you can optimize your study time and improve your overall exam performance. Remember to stay disciplined, adhere to your plan, and seek support when needed. With the power of proper study habits and a well-structured study plan, you can unlock your full learning potential and achieve academic excellence.

Reviewing and Consolidating Course Material

In order to fully grasp and retain the knowledge gained during your studies, it is crucial to review and consolidate the course material. Reviewing helps reinforce your understanding of the subject matter, while consolidation allows you to connect different concepts and create a comprehensive knowledge base. This subchapter will guide you through various techniques and strategies to effectively review and consolidate course material.

One of the most effective ways to review is by actively engaging with the material through techniques such as summarizing, highlighting key points, and creating flashcards. Summarizing allows you to condense complex information into concise, easy-to-understand statements. By doing so, you not only reinforce your understanding but also develop the ability to communicate the concepts clearly. Highlighting key points helps you identify the most important information in your course material, making it easier to review later. Flashcards are an excellent tool for memorization, as they force you to recall information and test your knowledge.

Consolidating course material involves connecting and integrating different concepts to form a coherent understanding of the subject. One effective strategy is to create concept maps or mind maps. These visual representations allow you to see the relationships between different ideas, helping you to better comprehend the overall structure and organization of the material. Additionally, teaching others is a powerful way to consolidate your knowledge. Explaining concepts to your classmates or even yourself in simple terms can reveal gaps in your understanding and solidify your grasp on the material.

Regularly scheduling review sessions is essential for long-term retention. Spacing out your review sessions over time, rather than cramming all at once, has been proven to enhance memory. Use tools such as calendars or planners to allocate dedicated time for reviewing course material. Setting specific goals for each review session will help you stay focused and motivated.

Remember, reviewing and consolidating course material is not a one-time task. It is an ongoing process that should be integrated into your study routine. By incorporating these strategies into your approach to learning, you will not only improve your understanding and retention of the material but also enhance your overall study habits.

Practicing with Past Exams and Sample Questions

In the journey towards academic success, one essential aspect often overlooked by students is the practice of solving past exams and sample questions. The significance of this practice cannot be emphasized enough, as it plays a pivotal role in maximizing your study habits and enhancing overall learning outcomes. By dedicating time to working on past exams and sample questions, you are equipping yourself with the necessary skills and knowledge to excel in your academic pursuits.

One of the key benefits of practicing with past exams and sample questions is that it allows you to familiarize yourself with the format and structure of the actual exams. Many students experience anxiety and stress when faced with exams, often stemming from the fear of the unknown. However, by engaging in regular practice sessions with past exams, you can overcome this fear and gain confidence in your abilities. Familiarity with the types of questions, time constraints, and overall expectations will enable you to approach the real exam with a calm and composed mindset.

Additionally, practicing with past exams and sample questions provides an excellent opportunity for self-assessment and evaluation of your knowledge and skills. Through this process, you can identify your strengths and weaknesses, allowing you to focus your efforts on areas that require improvement. By analyzing your performance, you can develop effective study strategies tailored to your specific needs. This targeted approach will not only enhance your understanding of the subject matter but also ensure that you make the most efficient use of your study time.

Moreover, solving past exams and sample questions helps you to develop critical thinking and problem-solving abilities. As you encounter different types of questions and scenarios, your ability to apply concepts and theories to real-world situations will improve significantly. This skill set is invaluable, not only for your academic success but also for your future professional endeavors.

In conclusion, incorporating the practice of solving past exams and sample questions into your study routine is crucial for maximizing your learning potential. It allows you to familiarize yourself with exam formats, evaluate your knowledge and skills, and develop critical thinking abilities. By dedicating time to this practice, you are equipping yourself with the tools necessary to excel academically and achieve your goals. Remember, practice makes perfect, and in the realm of education, it is the key to unlocking your true potential.

Managing Test Anxiety and Building Confidence

Test anxiety is a common experience among students, often leading to poor performance and a lack of confidence. However, with effective strategies and a positive mindset, it is possible to overcome this anxiety and build self-assurance in your abilities. This subchapter will explore various techniques to manage test anxiety and develop confidence, ultimately maximizing your study habits.

One of the key aspects of managing test anxiety is understanding its causes. Fear of failure, lack of preparation, and high expectations are often at the root of this anxiety. By acknowledging and addressing these underlying factors, you can begin to take control of your emotions and mindset.

To start, it is crucial to adopt effective study habits. This includes creating a study schedule, breaking down material into manageable chunks, and utilizing active learning techniques such as summarizing, self-quizzing, and teaching others. By being well-prepared, you can significantly reduce test anxiety.

Another essential strategy is practicing relaxation techniques. Deep breathing exercises, meditation, and progressive muscle relaxation are proven methods to calm the mind and body before a test. By incorporating these techniques into your study routine, you can create a sense of calmness and focus, promoting a positive test-taking experience.

Building confidence is equally important in managing test anxiety. One way to boost your self-assurance is by setting realistic goals and celebrating small victories along the way. By acknowledging your progress, you can build a positive self-image and believe in your abilities.

Additionally, positive self-talk and visualization can greatly impact your confidence. Replace negative thoughts with positive affirmations and visualize yourself successfully completing the test. This mental imagery will help reinforce your belief in your abilities and reduce anxiety.

Furthermore, seeking support from classmates, friends, or a mentor can provide you with an additional confidence boost. Discussing your concerns and sharing study strategies can help alleviate anxiety and provide a sense of camaraderie.

In conclusion, managing test anxiety and building confidence are crucial components of maximizing your study habits. By understanding the causes of test anxiety, adopting effective study habits, practicing relaxation techniques, and building self-assurance, you can overcome anxiety and perform at your best. Remember, test scores do not define your worth or intelligence. With the right mindset and strategies, you can conquer test anxiety and achieve academic success.

Chapter 8: Overcoming Study Challenges and Adapting to Learning Styles

Addressing Procrastination and Lack of Motivation

Procrastination and lack of motivation are two common challenges that many students face when it comes to studying. These obstacles can hinder academic success and prevent students from reaching their full potential. However, by understanding the root causes of these issues and implementing effective strategies, students can overcome procrastination and find the motivation they need to excel in their studies.

One of the main reasons why students procrastinate is because they feel overwhelmed by the tasks at hand. The sheer volume of assignments, projects, and exams can be daunting, leading to a sense of paralysis. To tackle this, it is important to break down larger tasks into smaller, more manageable ones. By creating a to-do list and prioritizing tasks, students can approach their workload in a more structured and organized manner. This not only helps to reduce feelings of overwhelm but also provides a sense of accomplishment as each task is completed.

Another common factor contributing to procrastination is the lack of clear goals and objectives. Without a clear direction, it is easy to lose motivation and become disengaged. Setting specific, measurable, achievable, relevant, and time-bound (SMART) goals can help students stay focused and motivated. By defining clear objectives, students have something tangible to work towards, which can reignite their enthusiasm for studying.

In addition to setting goals, creating a conducive study environment can play a significant role in combating procrastination. A cluttered or distracting workspace can easily divert attention and derail productivity. Designating a quiet and organized area for studying can help eliminate distractions and enhance concentration. Furthermore, incorporating elements such as natural light, comfortable seating, and inspiring décor can create a positive and inviting atmosphere that boosts motivation.

Sometimes, lack of motivation stems from a disconnection between students' interests and their studies. It is crucial for students to understand the relevance and importance of their academic pursuits. By finding personal connections to the subject matter, students can develop a genuine interest and intrinsic motivation to learn. Exploring real-life applications, connecting concepts to personal experiences, and seeking out mentors or role models in the field can foster a sense of excitement and curiosity.

In conclusion, addressing procrastination and lack of motivation is essential for students to maximize their study habits. By breaking tasks down, setting clear goals, creating a conducive study environment, and finding personal connections to the subject matter, students can overcome these obstacles and unlock their full academic potential. With the power of productive learning, students can transform their study habits and achieve outstanding results.

Tailoring Study Techniques to Individual Learning Styles

Subchapter: Tailoring Study Techniques to Individual Learning Styles

In the fast-paced world of academia, every student strives to achieve academic success. However, not all study techniques are created equal. Each student possesses a unique learning style, and tailoring your study techniques to suit your individual style can greatly enhance your productivity and comprehension. This subchapter explores the significance of understanding your learning style and provides effective strategies to maximize your study habits.

Understanding your learning style is essential in optimizing your study routine. Some students are visual learners, absorbing information through images and diagrams. Others are auditory learners, grasping concepts best through listening and discussions. Kinesthetic learners, on the other hand, learn best through hands-on experiences and physical activities. Recognizing your learning style enables you to adopt study techniques that align with your strengths, enabling you to absorb and retain information more effectively.

For visual learners, incorporating visual aids such as charts, mind maps, and color-coded notes can greatly enhance comprehension. Utilizing flashcards and creating visual mnemonics can also aid in remembering complex concepts. Auditory learners can benefit from recording lectures and listening to them repeatedly. Engaging in group discussions and explaining concepts aloud can reinforce understanding. Kinesthetic learners can integrate physical activities into their study routine, such as acting out scenarios or using manipulatives to understand abstract ideas.

Adapting your study environment to your learning style is equally important. Visual learners should ensure a well-lit space with minimal distractions, allowing them to focus on visual materials. Auditory learners can benefit from studying in quiet environments or using background music to enhance concentration. Kinesthetic learners may find it helpful to study in an active setting, incorporating movement or engaging in hands-on activities to facilitate learning.

Furthermore, it is essential to experiment with different study techniques to find what works best for you. Not all visual learners will respond to the same methods, and the same applies to auditory and kinesthetic learners. Keep a journal to track your progress and reflect on what techniques yield the most significant results.

Tailoring your study techniques to your individual learning style is a powerful tool for academic success. By understanding your unique strengths and preferences, you can create a study routine that maximizes productivity and comprehension. Embrace your learning style, experiment with various techniques, and watch as your study habits reach new heights. Remember, studying smarter, not harder, is the key to unlocking your full potential.

Dealing with Distractions and Maintaining Focus

In today's fast-paced world, distractions seem to be lurking around every corner, making it increasingly difficult for students to maintain focus and maximize their study habits. However, developing effective strategies to deal with these distractions is crucial to achieving academic success. In this subchapter, we will explore the importance of maintaining focus and provide practical tips on how to overcome distractions and stay on track with your studies.

Distractions can come in various forms, such as social media notifications, noisy environments, or even internal thoughts. These distractions can quickly derail your study sessions and hinder your ability to absorb and retain information effectively. Therefore, it is essential to establish a conducive study environment that minimizes interruptions. Find a quiet and comfortable space where you can concentrate without any disturbances. Consider using noise-cancelling headphones or playing instrumental music to block out external noise.

Another key aspect of dealing with distractions is self-discipline. Set specific goals for each study session and create a schedule that allows for regular breaks. During these breaks, give yourself permission to engage in activities that you find enjoyable or relaxing, such as going for a walk or reading a book. By incorporating these breaks into your study routine, you can reward yourself for maintaining focus during the designated study periods.

Furthermore, technology can be both a blessing and a curse when it comes to studying. While it provides access to vast amounts of information, it can also be a major distraction. To minimize the temptation of checking social media or browsing the internet aimlessly, consider using apps or browser extensions that block certain websites or limit your time spent on them.

Additionally, practicing mindfulness techniques can greatly enhance your ability to stay focused. Mindfulness involves being fully present and aware of your thoughts and surroundings. By practicing techniques such as deep breathing exercises or meditation before and during your study sessions, you can cultivate a sense of calm and improve your concentration.

In conclusion, dealing with distractions and maintaining focus is crucial for students who want to maximize their study habits. By creating a conducive study environment, practicing self-discipline, utilizing technology wisely, and incorporating mindfulness techniques, you can overcome distractions and achieve academic success. Remember, developing these skills will not only benefit your current studies but also equip you with valuable tools for lifelong learning. Stay focused, stay motivated, and embrace the power of productive learning.

Seeking Help and Support for Difficult Subjects

As students, we all encounter subjects that seem challenging and difficult to grasp. It's completely normal to struggle with certain topics or concepts, and it's important to remember that you are not alone in this journey. Seeking help and support when faced with difficult subjects is a crucial step in maximizing your study habits and achieving academic success.

The first thing to understand is that asking for help is not a sign of weakness or incompetence. In fact, it is quite the opposite. Recognizing your limitations and reaching out for assistance demonstrates maturity and a genuine desire to learn and improve. Remember, even the brightest minds seek guidance when faced with academic challenges.

One of the most effective ways to seek help is to approach your teachers or professors. They are there to support you and have a deep understanding of the subject matter. Don't hesitate to schedule a meeting or ask questions during class. Your educators will appreciate your initiative and dedication to understanding the material. They can explain concepts in different ways, provide additional resources, or suggest study strategies tailored to your learning style.

Another valuable resource is your peers. Form study groups with classmates who are also struggling with the same subject. Collaborating with others allows you to share ideas, discuss difficult topics, and gain different perspectives. Explaining concepts to each other is an excellent way to solidify your understanding and identify areas that need further clarification.

If you find it challenging to approach your teachers or form study groups, consider seeking help outside of your school. Tutoring centers, online platforms, or private tutors can provide personalized attention and guidance tailored to your specific needs. They can break down complex topics into manageable parts, provide practice exercises, and offer feedback on your progress.

Remember, seeking help and support is not limited to academic matters alone. If you find yourself overwhelmed or struggling emotionally due to the pressure of difficult subjects, don't hesitate to reach out to your school's counseling services. They can provide guidance on stress management, time management, and overall well-being.

In conclusion, seeking help and support for difficult subjects is a vital part of maximizing your study habits. It is a sign of strength and a commitment to your education. Utilize the resources available to you, be proactive in seeking assistance, and don't be afraid to ask questions. With the right support system, you can overcome any academic challenge and excel in your studies.

Chapter 9: The Role of Healthy Habits in Enhancing Study Performance

Importance of Proper Sleep for Cognitive Functioning

As students, it is common to prioritize our academic performance and study habits to excel in our studies. However, one crucial aspect that is often overlooked is the importance of proper sleep for cognitive functioning. In this subchapter, we will explore how getting adequate sleep can significantly impact our learning abilities and overall academic success.

Sleep plays a vital role in consolidating and retaining information. When we sleep, our brain goes through a process called memory consolidation, where it strengthens the neural connections associated with the knowledge and skills we have acquired throughout the day. This consolidation process is crucial for long-term memory formation, allowing us to recall information more effectively during exams or when needed.

Furthermore, proper sleep is directly linked to cognitive functions such as attention, concentration, and problem-solving. When we are well-rested, our brain functions optimally, enabling us to stay focused and absorb information more efficiently. On the other hand, a lack of sleep can lead to decreased attention span, impaired concentration, and reduced cognitive flexibility, hindering our ability to grasp complex concepts and perform well in exams.

Moreover, sleep deprivation has been shown to negatively affect our mood and emotional regulation. Lack of sleep can contribute to increased irritability, mood swings, and difficulty managing stress, all of which can significantly impact our ability to study effectively. By prioritizing proper sleep, we can improve our emotional well-being, leading to a more positive and productive study experience.

To ensure we get the most out of our sleep, it is essential to establish healthy sleep habits. Creating a consistent sleep schedule, where we go to bed and wake up at the same time every day, helps regulate our body's internal clock. Additionally, avoiding stimulants such as caffeine and electronic devices before bedtime can promote better sleep quality.

In conclusion, proper sleep is an integral part of maintaining optimal cognitive functioning. By recognizing the importance of sleep and prioritizing it alongside our study habits, we can enhance our learning abilities, memory retention, and overall academic performance. So, let us remember that a good night's sleep is not just a luxury but a necessity for students who strive for academic success.

Nutrition and Hydration: Fueling Your Brain for Learning

Proper study habits are essential for students to excel academically. However, what many students fail to realize is that their overall well-being, including their nutrition and hydration, plays a crucial role in optimizing their study habits and overall learning potential. In this subchapter, we will explore the importance of nutrition and hydration in fueling your brain for learning.

When it comes to maintaining a healthy and productive study routine, what you put into your body matters. Just like a car needs fuel to run efficiently, your brain needs the right nutrients to function at its best. A balanced diet rich in fruits, vegetables, whole grains, and lean proteins provides your brain with the essential vitamins and minerals it needs to perform optimally. Incorporating brain-boosting foods such as blueberries, fatty fish, nuts, and seeds can enhance memory, concentration, and cognitive function.

Additionally, staying hydrated is crucial for maintaining optimal brain function. Dehydration can lead to fatigue, poor concentration, and decreased cognitive abilities. Make sure to drink enough water throughout the day to keep your brain hydrated and functioning at its peak. Avoid excessive consumption of sugary drinks and caffeine as they can lead to energy crashes and hinder your ability to focus.

Furthermore, timing your meals and snacks strategically can help you maintain steady energy levels throughout the day. Eating small, frequent meals or snacks that include a combination of complex carbohydrates, protein, and healthy fats can sustain your energy and prevent you from experiencing dips in concentration. Avoid relying on sugary snacks or processed foods, as they can cause energy crashes and negatively impact your ability to retain information.

Incorporating proper nutrition and hydration into your study routine not only improves your brain's performance but also enhances your overall well-being. A healthy body promotes a healthy mind, and by taking care of your physical needs, you are setting yourself up for success in your academic pursuits.

In conclusion, nutrition and hydration are vital components of optimizing your study habits and maximizing your learning potential. By fueling your brain with a balanced diet, staying hydrated, and timing your meals strategically, you can enhance your focus, memory, and cognitive abilities. Remember, taking care of your physical well-being is just as important as developing effective study habits. So, make conscious choices about what you eat and drink, and watch as your productivity and academic performance soar to new heights.

Incorporating Physical Activity for Mental Clarity

In today's fast-paced and demanding academic environment, students often find themselves overwhelmed with the pressure to excel in their studies. Developing effective study habits is crucial for success, but it is equally important to understand the role of physical activity in achieving mental clarity. This subchapter delves into the significance of incorporating physical activity into your routine to enhance productivity and optimize your study habits.

Physical activity has been proven to have numerous benefits for the brain. Engaging in regular exercise increases blood flow to the brain, delivering essential nutrients and oxygen that enhance cognitive function. It also stimulates the release of neurotransmitters, such as dopamine and serotonin, which are associated with improved mood and focus. By incorporating physical activity into your daily routine, you can effectively combat the mental fatigue and stress often experienced during intense study sessions.

One effective way to incorporate physical activity into your study routine is by taking short breaks throughout your study sessions. Instead of succumbing to the temptation of mindlessly scrolling through social media, use these breaks to engage in physical activities that get your blood pumping. It could be as simple as a brisk walk around your campus or a quick stretching routine. Not only will this rejuvenate your mind but also improve your overall well-being.

Another effective method is to schedule dedicated time for physical activity. Allocate specific time slots in your daily or weekly schedule for activities such as jogging, swimming, or attending fitness classes.

This not only ensures that you prioritize physical activity but also provides a well-deserved break from studying, allowing your brain to recharge. Additionally, engaging in group activities or team sports can also provide the added benefits of social interaction and stress relief, further enhancing your mental clarity.

Remember, physical activity and mental clarity go hand in hand. By incorporating regular exercise into your study routine, you can improve your focus, memory, and overall cognitive abilities. It is important to find physical activities that you enjoy and that fit into your schedule. Experiment with different forms of exercise until you find the ones that resonate with you. By making physical activity a priority, you will not only maximize your study habits but also improve your overall well-being. So, lace up your sneakers, grab your workout gear, and get ready to unleash the power of physical activity for enhanced mental clarity and productive learning.

Stress Management Techniques for a Balanced Mindset

As students, we often find ourselves overwhelmed with the pressures of academic life. From deadlines and exams to extracurricular activities and social commitments, it's no wonder that stress and anxiety can start to take a toll on our mental well-being. However, by implementing effective stress management techniques, we can maintain a balanced mindset and improve our overall study habits.

One of the most important aspects of stress management is recognizing the signs of stress and taking proactive steps to address it. Some common symptoms of stress include difficulty concentrating, feeling overwhelmed or irritable, and experiencing physical symptoms such as headaches or stomachaches. By being aware of these signals, we can intervene early on and prevent stress from hindering our productivity.

One powerful stress management technique is engaging in regular physical activity. Exercise has been proven to release endorphins, which are natural mood elevators, and reduce stress hormones in the body. Whether it's going for a run, joining a sports team, or practicing yoga, finding a form of exercise that you enjoy can have a significant impact on your stress levels and overall well-being.

Another effective technique is practicing mindfulness and relaxation exercises. This can include deep breathing exercises, meditation, or engaging in activities that promote relaxation, such as listening to calming music or taking a warm bath. By incorporating these practices into our daily routine, we can train our minds to stay present and focused, reducing stress and increasing our ability to concentrate on our studies.

Additionally, time management skills play a crucial role in stress management. By creating a realistic study schedule and setting achievable goals, we can prevent last-minute cramming sessions and the associated stress that comes with them. Prioritizing tasks, breaking them down into smaller, manageable steps, and scheduling regular breaks can help us maintain a balanced workload and prevent burnout.

Lastly, seeking support from friends, family, or even professional counselors can provide invaluable assistance in managing stress. Sometimes, simply talking about our worries and concerns can help alleviate the burden and provide us with fresh perspectives and potential solutions.

By implementing these stress management techniques, students can cultivate a balanced mindset and enhance their study habits. Remember, managing stress is not about eliminating it entirely, but rather finding healthy coping mechanisms that allow us to navigate the challenges of academic life with resilience and mental clarity.

Chapter 10: Sustaining Long-Term Study Habits for Lifelong Learning

Developing a Growth Mindset for Continuous Improvement

In the pursuit of academic success, it is essential for students to cultivate a growth mindset that fosters continuous improvement. This subchapter delves into the significance of developing such a mindset and its direct correlation with establishing effective study habits. By embracing a growth mindset, students can unlock their true potential and excel in their educational journey.

A growth mindset is the belief that intelligence and abilities can be developed through dedication, effort, and a willingness to learn from failure. It is a fundamental mindset shift that empowers students to see challenges as opportunities for growth rather than obstacles to overcome. Embracing this mindset allows students to approach their studies with resilience, adaptability, and a hunger for knowledge.

One of the key benefits of adopting a growth mindset is the ability to persevere through setbacks. When faced with difficult concepts or challenging assignments, students with a growth mindset view these moments as valuable learning experiences. They understand that failure is not an endpoint but a stepping stone towards improvement. By maintaining a positive attitude and seeking support when needed, students can overcome obstacles and achieve academic success.

Another advantage of developing a growth mindset is the motivation to embrace continuous learning. Students who believe that their abilities can be developed are more likely to take ownership of their education and seek out opportunities for growth. They actively engage in self-reflection, identify areas of improvement, and actively seek strategies to enhance their study habits. This proactive approach leads to enhanced learning outcomes and a deeper understanding of the subject matter.

To develop a growth mindset, students can start by reframing their perception of failure. Instead of viewing failure as a personal deficiency, students can see it as an opportunity for growth and learning. They can reflect on their mistakes, identify areas for improvement, and adjust their study strategies accordingly.

Furthermore, students can foster a growth mindset by embracing challenges and seeking out intellectually stimulating experiences. By stepping out of their comfort zones and tackling difficult tasks, students can develop resilience, problem-solving skills, and a sense of accomplishment.

Finally, developing a growth mindset requires students to cultivate a positive and supportive learning environment. Surrounding themselves with peers who also strive for growth and seek improvement will create a culture that encourages collaboration, reflection, and intellectual curiosity.

In conclusion, developing a growth mindset is essential for students seeking continuous improvement in their academic journey. By adopting this mindset, students can overcome setbacks, embrace challenges, and develop effective study habits. By viewing failure as an opportunity for growth and maintaining a positive attitude, students can unlock their full potential and achieve academic success.

Setting Long-Term Goals and Tracking Progress

In the journey of academic success, setting long-term goals and tracking your progress is of paramount importance. This subchapter will delve into the significance of establishing clear objectives and monitoring your advancement towards them, helping you maximize your study habits and ultimately achieve your desired outcomes.

Long-term goals provide direction and purpose to your academic endeavors. They give you a roadmap to follow, ensuring that you stay focused and motivated throughout your educational journey. By setting specific, measurable, attainable, relevant, and time-bound (SMART) goals, you create a framework that allows you to make progress in a systematic and organized manner.

When setting long-term goals, it is crucial to align them with your personal aspirations and values. Reflect on what you truly want to achieve academically and why it matters to you. By understanding the underlying motivations behind your goals, you can cultivate a deeper sense of commitment and dedication, making the journey towards them more meaningful and fulfilling.

Once you have established your long-term goals, it is essential to break them down into smaller, manageable tasks. This helps to prevent overwhelm and allows you to focus on one step at a time. By breaking your goals into smaller milestones, you can track your progress more effectively, celebrating each achievement along the way and staying motivated for the next step.

Tracking your progress is an integral part of the learning process. Regularly reviewing your advancement not only helps you stay on track but also enables you to identify areas that may require additional attention. It allows you to assess the effectiveness of your study habits and make necessary adjustments to optimize your learning experience.

There are various methods for tracking progress, such as maintaining a study journal, using a task management app, or creating a visual tracking system. Find a method that resonates with you and suits your learning style, ensuring that it is easy to use and provides a clear overview of your progress.

Remember, setting long-term goals and tracking your progress is not just about achieving academic success; it is about cultivating lifelong learning habits. By adopting these practices, you develop valuable skills such as self-discipline, time management, and self-reflection, which will serve you well beyond your educational journey.

In conclusion, the process of setting long-term goals and tracking your progress is a powerful tool for maximizing your study habits. By establishing clear objectives, breaking them down into manageable tasks, and regularly monitoring your advancement, you can stay focused, motivated, and on track towards achieving academic success. Embrace the importance of proper study habits and leverage the power of goal-setting to unlock your full potential.

Embracing Lifelong Learning and Seeking Further Education

In today's fast-paced and rapidly evolving world, the importance of proper study habits cannot be overstated. As students, we find ourselves constantly grappling with new information, technologies, and methodologies. To keep up with these changes and excel in our academic and professional pursuits, it is crucial to embrace lifelong learning and seek further education.

Lifelong learning is the process of acquiring knowledge and skills throughout one's life, beyond the formal education years. It is a mindset that recognizes the value of continuous growth and development. By adopting this approach, we open ourselves up to endless possibilities and opportunities for personal and professional advancement.

One of the key benefits of embracing lifelong learning is that it allows us to stay current and relevant in our chosen fields. The knowledge and skills acquired during our formal education may become outdated over time, given the rapid pace of innovation and change. By actively seeking further education, we can bridge these gaps and ensure that we remain at the forefront of our industries.

Moreover, lifelong learning fosters a growth mindset, which is essential for success in any endeavor. It encourages us to embrace challenges, persist in the face of setbacks, and continuously improve ourselves. As we engage in lifelong learning, we develop resilience, adaptability, and the ability to think critically. These qualities not only enhance our academic performance but also equip us with the tools to navigate the complexities of the real world.

Additionally, seeking further education beyond the traditional classroom setting provides us with valuable exposure to diverse perspectives and experiences. Through workshops, seminars, online courses, and professional development programs, we can broaden our horizons and gain new insights. This exposure enables us to become well-rounded individuals and helps us develop a deeper understanding of the world around us.

In conclusion, the subchapter on embracing lifelong learning and seeking further education emphasizes the importance of continuously expanding our knowledge and skills. By adopting a growth mindset and actively pursuing opportunities for learning, we can stay relevant, develop essential qualities for success, and broaden our perspectives. In this ever-changing world, lifelong learning is not only a means to excel academically but also a pathway to personal and professional fulfillment. Embrace the power of lifelong learning and unlock your true potential.

Cultivating a Positive Attitude Towards Learning

In today's fast-paced world, acquiring knowledge and skills is more critical than ever. As students, it is essential to develop a positive attitude towards learning to maximize your study habits and achieve academic success. In this subchapter, we will explore the significance of cultivating a positive attitude towards learning and how it can enhance your overall educational experience.

A positive attitude towards learning sets the foundation for effective study habits. When you approach your studies with enthusiasm and a growth mindset, you are more likely to be motivated and engaged in the learning process. Instead of viewing learning as a chore, consider it as an opportunity for personal growth and development. Embrace the challenges that come with learning, as they provide valuable opportunities to expand your knowledge and skills.

Maintaining a positive attitude towards learning also helps in overcoming obstacles and setbacks. As students, you will inevitably face difficulties along your academic journey. However, by adopting a positive mindset, you can see challenges as opportunities for learning and growth rather than as roadblocks. With a positive attitude, you will be more resilient and better equipped to overcome obstacles and bounce back from setbacks.

A positive attitude towards learning also enhances your ability to absorb and retain information. When you approach your studies with a positive mindset, you are more likely to be focused and attentive, allowing you to grasp concepts more effectively. Additionally, a positive attitude can improve your memory and recall abilities, making it easier for you to retain information for exams and assignments.

Moreover, cultivating a positive attitude towards learning fosters a love for knowledge. When you view learning as an enjoyable and fulfilling process, you are more likely to develop a lifelong passion for learning. This thirst for knowledge will extend beyond the classroom and into your personal and professional life, enabling you to continuously grow and adapt to new challenges and opportunities.

In conclusion, cultivating a positive attitude towards learning is crucial for students aiming to maximize their study habits and succeed academically. By approaching learning with enthusiasm, embracing challenges, and maintaining a growth mindset, you can enhance your overall educational experience. A positive attitude towards learning not only improves your motivation and engagement but also helps you overcome obstacles, retain information, and develop a lifelong love for knowledge. Remember, a positive mindset is a powerful tool that can unlock your full potential and lead you to academic success.